OVER DESOTO'S BONES

by
Conger Beasley, Jr.

Ahsahta Press

Boise State University
Boise, Idaho

Poems selected and edited by Orvis C. Burmaster

Second Printing, March 1984

ISBN 0-916272-11-7

Library of Congress Catalog Card Number:
78-74299

for John Carroll
1919-1974

Contents

Introduction

This volume is an adept mixture of fact/history, surrealism, and mysticism. Beasley begins with Anza's **Memoirs**, so "scandalous" that in the edition I read whole pages were never translated by the scholar who edited them, but left in the original Spanish. Not that Anza intended it that way—it's just that the tribes he was describing (factually) were so far outside the norms of the civilized that prudish Berkeley professors didn't know what to do with them. And Beasley captures that mostly-funny sense of "barbarism" that Anza confronted in the Colorado Desert (and the rest of the Southwest). Only then comes the surrealism, or better (in line with the Big Tradition in contemporary Latin America, including Brazil), Magic Realism. Anza takes a shit; "the turds slide out easily./ As he hitches up his baggy trousers/ a flower blooms, a spring gushes, a city erupts/ on a spot no bigger than a cracked egg." It's Asturias, Marquez, the Brasilian Murilo Rubião.

Then the mysticism, or let's call it magic, maybe not Magic Realism, as a literary device, but real magic, as a way of life:

> Pedro Alvarez learned all sorts of magic from the little blue book.
> He learned to see in the dark
> by biting the head off a bat
> and rubbing the blood on his eyelids.
> . . . .
>
> He learned how to become invisible
> by cooking a black cat in an *olla*
> and chewing the bones.

All tricks of a Yaqui medicine man. You can feel the presence of Castaneda's Don Juan here.

It's interesting to see how neatly pre-Columbian magic melds with very contemporary literary tricks—it's a straining for Beyond Pragmatism. Magic (technique or "fact") is really a re-affirmation of the power of spirit—and that's what this book is filled with, a plea for authenticity that isn't Hollywood ("Approaches to Splendor"), isn't racist ("The Zoot-Suit War"), isn't practical or sensible ("Harry Truman Takes a Walk"), in fact that plugs into one of the oldest visions of the so-called New World, the New World as the "Hell" of the Old World:

You have entered the oldest country,
an infernal region of memory
& desire. Perhaps you thought
you were in Hell?

In a way Beasley is like Hart Crane in **The Bridge**, contrasting the new, the modern, the efficient, the scientific, with old, primitive magic. Magic versus Science. The "New" World standing humming in its "magicness," and then Europe begins to invade, and across centuries the magic terminates in Harry Truman the A-Bomb Astronaut.

Why call the last section about DeSoto's bones (more echoes of **The Bridge**) "An Initiation Story"? Because DeSoto becomes the prototype of the changeover/initiation of European into "Indian." The dead DeSoto over the centuries has become a shaman:

SHAZAM, BOY! Hernando boomed

& instantly each bone ignited like an albino eye
lighting up this murky world

a hundred different myriad lights
for me, at least, to see.

"For me, at least, to see" — the point of the whole book, an invitation to a "visioning."

Hugh Fox
Santa Catarina Island, Brazil
March, 1979

Sonora

At midday nothing moves.
Shadows are crowded with creatures
visible only to one another.
Everything else is missing: rocks, rivers, valleys, mountains, mesas,
    missions.
Step out of a shadow and you disappear. For people
these shadows are umbilical connections to ferny civilizations.
Squatting in a shadow a man can imagine pine trees girdling a green lake.
A shadow offers a funnel into depths
where pupfish jabber familiar dialects
and rivers cough up wet stones.
In Sonora everything is invisible
until it impinges upon a shadow:
a lizard does not see the hawk
until the hawk is upon him
and he is flung out into the sun.
Phantoms do not materialize until they are touched by shadows;
the hawk is not real until the lizard dreams it.

Approaches to Splendor:
Ferde Grofé, 1921

Ferde Grofé looks over the Grand Canyon.
It is sunset, the sky like a wine flagon streaked with vintage colors.
Some cut, he whispers. This canyon reaches deeper
than the tentacles of a giant squid.
I will gloss over it with a thin brush,
highlighting here, shading there,
so the image of the original will not be muddled
by a surrogate. Surrogates are clumsy anyway,
opaque prisms interposed between the eye and hallowed object.
Art requires the deftest touch to limn what is already there:
Subtle magnification of unimpeachable sources.

Anza Conquers the Desert

Note:

The first white man to enter the Colorado Desert was Melchior Diaz in the 1540s. The earth trembled, the sand was hot as ashes, the country desolate and forbidding. He stayed four days and returned to Mexico.

For the next 200 years the desert remained the domain of the Indian. Jesuit missions were established in Baja California and Northern Sonora, while the Franciscans colonized Alta California along the Pacific coast. In 1774, Captain Juan Bautista de Anza led an expedition from San Xavier del Bac near Tucson into the Colorado Desert.

The time had come to link the mission system by land.

1

Anza showed no one the map.
Traced on parchment,
He studied it alone every night
by the fire.
The big river marked in the center
pulsed like the vein in the neck
of an hysteric woman:

> *Follow me*
> *& you will choke;*
>
> *cross me & you will drown.*

2

The first natives Anza encountered
were so wretched
they followed vultures
to rob them of their prey.
The only animal they would not eat
was the badger
because it resembled them
in looks & fierceness.
Cannibalism was the only vice
they did not cultivate.
When meat was scarce
they tied a piece to a string
by which it was retrieved from their stomachs
again & again.
When cactus fruit was in season
they gorged themselves;
when the season passed
they picked the seeds from their own excrement
& ate them.
Though they possessed bows & arrows
they were unskilled hunters
& lived on what they could pick up:
lizards, locusts, spiders, caterpillars,
the lice from their own hair.

3

The column halts, the horses are hobbled,
sweaty blankets spread out to dry.
A fire is started, beef jerky hauled out of saddlebags.
With the dying sun in his eyes
Anza defecates on the ground.
Despite the long day's ride
the turds slide out easily.
As he hitches up his baggy trousers
a flower blooms, a spring gushes, a city erupts
on a spot no bigger than a cracked egg.

Anza rushes back to the fire
to tell the others.

4

The stink of creosote
reminds him of his wife's wetness
on his thighs.
No snake can tongue it off;
the hide of a horned toad
vigorously applied
proves fruitless.
I am tainted, he thinks;
stained to the marrow.
Not even the water of the ocean
can wash me clean.
Desert blight, woman stench...
I must hoard my semen
for struggles yet to come.

5

Columbus said the world was like a pear
with a stalk, or projection, at the tip
like a woman's nipple.

The desert is a sheet of armor
fired white & hammered flat.

There is a kettle & over there a pot;
a tongue beckons from the arroyo.

The heat makes us transparent
incorporeal as ghosts.

Our bones glow like silk cords.

Sergeant Alvarez looked into the sun one afternoon
& disappeared, a column of shrieking light
you could gallop a horse through.

Even Columbus would have lost his way in this glare.
With no stalk to mount or nipple to suck
he would have found the edge & plummeted over.

6

Anza covers his eyes. Proud man
roweled by the fiery spurs of God!
Thoughts of sex dwindle to a ball of spit.
Even violence loses its savor.
The taste of blood grows rancid.
Bones loosen, arms & legs crumble
like the leaves of a paloverde tree.
It is so hot. It is so lonely. It is so awful.
A Spaniard doesn't need a conscience here.
He needs a nose, two ears, a stomach like a worm
& heavy claws to burrow away from the sun.

7

Sand swirling in blizzard force
drove them off their horses.
A soldier from Extremadura
thought it was snow.
He stripped off his clothes
& ran out of the corral,
squealing with delight.
Hours later they found him
eyes sanded over, nostrils and throat clotted
with grainy particles,
hands cupped like a beggar's
in a village market on festival day.

8

Stars radiate an eerie knowledge,
encyclopedia of icy waves
that break soundlessly
against Anza's sleeping face.
A kangaroo rat hopping across the fire
is stunned by their message
& falls into the coals.
At dawn Anza wakes up refreshed
& bounds across the desert
toward distant blue-black mountains
like a puma toward a wounded buffalo.

9

The only woman they saw
was a dead one. A Yuma
had split her crotch open
& removed the lips of her vulva
(surgically, with a stone knife)
& was wearing them around the village
speaking mysterious gibberish.

10

Anza dreams of ancient seas.
His spurs uproot old fossils.
The mark of a former shoreline is visible on a far-off mountain.
Fish nudge his parched eyes.
Pterodactyls dip their beaks with the ease of bats.
A thunderhead deluges his crackling hair.
A friendly Papago offers a fresh wound to suck.
One by one his men flounder in the sand.
Pack mules bray for respite.
Bony memorabilia chalk the trail.

Wearily Anza pisses
vowing revenge against the sun.

11

Whiteness is purity.
Whiteness is strength.
Whiteness is immortality.

Indians are colored.
Rocks are colored.
Mountains are colored.

Only the sun at midday
burning & unbearable
is white.

At noon Anza halts the column
& orders his men to take off their helmets
& stare into the sky.

12

I can swim in sand, said Lieutenant Mimbres.
Sand is really a liquid
coarser, less refined
but navigable by a strong man with desire.
He stripped to his tunic & plunged in.
For about a mile the lieutenant swam
with an easy overarm crawl
till he bumped against a rock
& called for help.
The others pulled him out
& administered first aid:
thorns & whiptails with a vengeance
to cure him of his foolishness.

13

Resplendent
in a gown fashioned
from the tail feathers
of a hundred-thousand
ruby-throated hummingbirds,
the Pima chief levitates toward them
on feet sandaled
with the hymens
of a dozen sacrificial
virgins.

14

They split open so many skulls that afternoon
their wrists & faces were stained bright red.
Lopped limbs coiled in the dust like frenzied snakes.
Days later the air in the village was still damp.
A good scourging, thought Father Garcés
as he blessed each hut with a torch.

15

Bats invade Anza's beard.
He caresses them with his fingertips.
Later he installs a couple in his pubic hair.
Near his aching testicles the bats encounter hostile vermin.
So fierce is the battle Anza pitches & rolls all night.
By the light of the false dawn he is discovered by Father Garcés
humping his saddlebags & calling out the name
of a favorite whore in Tubac.

16

God is an illusion, said Father Garcés
                    in a friendly after-dinner discussion.
He is the antithesis of the rocks & mountains that block our path.
They can be removed, torn down, shoved aside.
God is not a thing; God is a spirit, a presence, an idea.
We get close to Him by unburdening ourselves
                        of excess physical baggage.
Like milkweed we are blown by the wind till we no longer remember
                                what we were.
Even then we don't find God; we lose our senses.
God is beyond our madness, beyond our hunger to dissolve.

17

Anza rides across the desert.
Pellucid light illuminates a sidewinder on a mountain ten miles away.

Anza reins in.
Is that the sea? he wonders.
A group of Papagos hauling salt to Tubac pauses nearby.
A wraith-like figure, encumbered with beard & hauberk,
rises off the sand.

Is that a cactus? they wonder.
Past one another they shimmer, at parade rest.
California beckons; for Arizona, statehood is a century-and-a-half away.

Illusions persist, ancient paintings in the air
gilding rocks & cactus
before moving on.

The Lizard

A Cahuilla Indian tale

Once there was a man named Tameotemevai.
He could do incredible things.
He could rip open his stomach with a knife & feel no pain.
The wound would heal up without a scar.
He could fill a pipe with tobacco & hold it up to the sun.
Smoke would curl out the bowl.
He could pull his tongue two feet out of his mouth.
He liked to strut around the village & crack it over people's heads.
One day Tameotemevai's wife ran away from him.
He found her in a neighboring village.
He tried to beat her but the men in the village wouldn't let him.
Tameotemevai sneered at them.
When he tried to drag his wife away
they hit him with clubs & knocked him down.
Then they jumped on him & tore his body to pieces.
Several times before they had killed him
& always Tameotemevai had come back to life.
This time they ripped open his body & a lizard jumped out of his heart.
The men chased the lizard around the village & finally caught it.
They buried it as far underground as they could dig.
Soon there was an earthquake.
It was the lizard trying to get out
& put the pieces of Tameotemevai's body back together again.
It did not succeed.

Approaches to Splendor:
Zane Grey, 1907

Buffalo Jones
a feisty coot
made the perfect ciceroni.
He led Zane
over terrain
few white eyes
had ever seen.
See that? said Buffalo
pointing to a mountain
75 miles away;
almost like you
could touch it
with your hand.
Zane couldn't
and so computed
the distance
to a different scale
and peopled it
with faces
Fenimore Cooper
would have approved.
Old Buffalo
knew better;
all those years
grubbing with Indians
had colored his vision
till he could detect
forces other
than what his imagination
conjured:
ominous phantoms
that blew past Zane
ruffling his hair
and swelling his nostrils
but leaving his white eyes
unmarked.

Pedro Alvarez
1

Pedro Alvarez was a witch; his father Anesto had been a witch.
Only a witch can use a magic cigarette.
A magic cigarette is made from a special tobacco called *hiacbibam*
that grows high up in the Sierras.
The story of *hiacbibam* is interesting.
Long ago there was an ugly woman.
She was the ugliest woman in the world.
No one loved her.
In despair she went to a wise man
and asked what she could do to make people like her.
The wise man told her he could turn her into tobacco
and every time a man smoked a cigarette
he would caress her.

Note:
"Pedro Alvarez" is drawn from **A Yaqui Life**, a book of reminiscences by
Rosalio Moisés.

2

Pedro Alvarez liked to play with magic cigarettes.
One night he wrapped some *hiacbibam* in a cornhusk.
The cigarette was about six inches long
and big around as his little finger.
Pedro told the cigarette to fly out in the desert
and look around. He lit the cigarette
and sucked on it three times.
There was a pop like an engine backfiring
and the cigarette took off across the desert.
Pedro could see it bobbing between the cactus like a firefly.
Half an hour later the cigarette returned
and whispered in Pedro's ear
about as loud as a buzzing mosquito.
The place where it had been was dark
and there was nothing to see.

3

A bad witch can kill a person with a magic cigarette.
Lino Sopomea was killed this way in 1923.
One night Lino played cards with a bunch of Papagos
and won all their money.
One of the Papagos was a witch.
The next day as Lino was crossing the street
a magic cigarette struck him in the neck.
Lino thought he had been stung by a bee.
He put cold water on his neck and forgot about it.
The next day he was dead.

4

Pedro Alvarez had a book that he kept with him always.
It was a little blue book with a pleasant odor.
He liked to read the book and repeat the *oraciones*.
If you make a mistake repeating the *oraciones*
the magic you want may backfire and cause you harm.
But Pedro Alvarez never made a mistake.
One time he was captured by three Mexicans and put in jail.
The Mexicans were going to kill him because he was a Yaqui.
That night after whispering the *oraciones*
he opened the iron gate of his cell;
the Mexicans stood like they were frozen.
Pedro took a gun and ammunition and a canteen.
No dog barked as he walked out of the jail.

5

Pedro Alvarez learned all sorts of magic from the little blue book.
He learned to see in the dark
by biting the head off a bat
and rubbing the blood on his eyelids.
He learned how to be a good cowboy
by biting the head off a hummingbird
and stashing the feathers
in a little bag under his vest.
He learned how to become invisible
by cooking a black cat in an *olla*
and chewing the bones.

6

Pedro Alvarez kept a *chone* in his house.
A *chone* is a scalp
or a doll to which a scalp is attached.
A *chone* can fly through the air like a magic cigarette.
Yaqui soldiers in the Sierra liked to take a *chone* along
because the *chone* could scout ahead
and signal when they were in danger.
A bad witch can kill a person with a *chone*.
The *chone* flies through the air
and wraps itself around the person's neck
and strangles them.
A *chone* sent out by a bad witch is a frightening thing.
If you hear a whispering noise in your house
look sharp for a *chone*.
Throw ashes and ground chili on it right away;
the *chone* will get scared and fly back to the witch
and never return.

7

31

One night Pedro Alvarez lay on his cot
and repeated the *oraciones* for flying.
His body stayed on the cot
while his spirit flew around the village
tapping on window panes
and dropping gravel on rooftops.
The next night the *mayordomo* led a search for the phantom.
Pedro Alvarez helped. He thought it very funny
to be out in the streets looking for himself.
The following night he flew around the village
scaring more people.
But he never hurt anyone. He just wanted to have fun.

Desert Events

for Barry Holstun Lopez

1

Sit in a shadow.
Compress your eyes to slits.
Breathe lightly.
Let your pores dilate till the light swells your limbs.
Float up to a palm tree.
Bask in a frond.
At sunset your pores will contract, your limbs deflate.
Emptied of light you will drift back down.

2

Find an oasis. Go there.
A horsefly will challenge you.
Stand still & let him bump you.
Approach the oasis. Sit.
Locate the point where you hear water.
Cup your hands.
The fly will bump you again.
Drink together.

3

Go out when a full moon is rising.
Face east.
Run your hands over your face & chest.
Make the same soaping motions three nights running.
When the moon disappears your body will glow with light.

4

Go to a spot where you are completely alone.
Forget your name, your age, your weight.
Take your voice out of your throat & stick it in the sand.
Try to imagine yourself without a face.
Walk backwards into the landscape until you disappear.

5

Come down from a mountain & pick up a rock.
Spit on it.
Replace it & walk out of sight.
Turn around & shield your eyes.
Remain motionless as a lizard.
A waterfall will appear on the horizon.

6

Stand under a palm tree on a moonless night.
Press your cheek against the trunk.
Close your eyes.
Breathe through your nose.
Feel the stars crackle against your teeth.

7

Make friends with a mockingbird.
Offer it food & water.
When the bird sings mimic the sound.
Practice this often.
When you reach the point where you fool the mockingbird
walk out of your house & never go back.

An Original Dime Novel

Jack rides west. Shortly after dawn. Sun gaping like a hawk. Mesquite greasy with dew. Wood doves gargling in the slick branches. Across flat plains etched with brittle shadows Jack guides his faithful mount. Morning unlimbers to a chorus of grouse, a crow hawking from a ridge. Gophers chitter in gossipy pairs. A geyser erupts from a natural well. At noon the air thickens, forming a crust on Jack's fingers. He pauses to chew. Three Comanches try to peel his scalp. Jack sticks two and guts the third. Jerks the pieces over a flame. A buzzard drops in and is bountifully rewarded. The wind licks Jack's ears. Ghost country, a border reach between Comanche and Kiowa. Holes through which phantoms leak in the guise of garrulous coots. Jack packs his ears with wax and sallies on. Late after-noon clouds spell a curious script. Jack knows the sign; he's been this way before. A saloon appears. Clyde. A saloon and a jumble of shacks. Thirst swells his tongue. Inside, the joint is crammed. Jack knocks back a whiskey. Another. Muleteers crowd the bar. Aint you Jack Crack? Am. Am. Whar you bound? Up your ass; I hear the pickins are good. A fist clips Jack's chin. He oughten to drink without a coating of beans. Outside, the street tilts west to catch the last flicker of light before night lowers like an awning and bats pick the lice from his hair. Jack gulps a plate of rice. A floozie perks up her skirt. His ass is sore, his head aches, but he can still holler. Upstairs, he makes big tracks across her belly. Snorting like a dinosaur. Later he's waylaid by a pair of wastrels looking for a Wells Fargo dick. Jack spikes one, garottes the other with his thumb. Sleeps at last, sweet as a pup. A fat moon balms the dust. Coyotes sleepwalk over roofs. An owl lumbers home with a talon full of trophies. Somewhere a rooster croaks. The floozie wakes; Jack pulps out another bolt and rinses his jowls. .44 clamped to his hip, he lopes for the stall. His horse nickers. Another day. Jack rides.

Approaches to Splendor: Cecil B. DeMille, 1915

Clad in jodphurs, leather boots,
a revolver strapped to his hip,
Cecil B. strides onto the set.
Suddenly you can hear a gnat squeak.
What I want is simple,
he says to his assembled minions;
I want to erect a tower so tall
that from its vantage point
I will be able to direct
the influx of immigrants
looking to make California
their permanent home.
They will *need* direction; the air
out here is not like it is
back in Philadelphia,
and they will be confused at first
and befuddled.
With the sharp enclosures magically removed
a whole new world of horizontal possibilities
will open up for them
and they will be prone to melancholy
and fits of weeping.
I know; I am an immigrant too,
and when immigrants step off a boat
even in the middle of the desert
they are discombobulated
and need something to fasten onto.
Rocks and cacti are too hostile;
immigrants need images commensurate
with their longing for the past,
and these images I will give them
by the barrelful:
bearded images and saintly images,
hooded images and knavely images;
a vision of the Old World in Biblical garb,
a European version of conqueror and slave,

which they in turn will reproject
in a million kinetic fragments
onto the natural features of this alien land
till what was once real in the rocks and cacti
will be virtually unrecognizable....

The Zoot-Suit War

"Race does not lie in the language but exclusively in the blood."
— Adolph Hitler

1

Perhaps it was the dress that gave offense:
girls wore tight sweaters, short skirts, and pompadours;
boys wore high-waisted, peg-legged pants
with loose, wide-shouldered coats:
zoot suits, they were called.
With wide-brimmed hats and droopy key chains
the costume was similar
to what the *vaqueros* wore in the old rancho days
before the Anglos arrived
and California belonged to Mexico.

2

The boys who wore these suits were called *pachucos*.
Their fathers had respected the boundaries of the Mexican community
but their sons declared themselves Americans
and wandered far away from the *barrios*
into the downtown shopping districts,
the beaches, Hollywood.
Instead of their fathers' anonymity
they wanted to be identified for what they were
and so adopted as their uniform the drape-shape
or zoot-suit
which made it easy for the police to round them up
and work them over.

3

In an official explanation of *pachuco* delinquency
published in 1942
the Los Angeles County sheriff's office declared:
"The Caucasian when engaged in fighting
resorts to fisticuffs and may kick,
which is considered unsportive; but this Mexican element
considers this a sign of weakness.
All he feels is a desire to use a knife.
His desire is to kill, or let blood....
When liquor is added to this inborn characteristic
we have crimes of violence...."

4

Sleepy Lagoon was an irrigation ditch in Montebello
where Mexican-Americans went to swim.
Denied access to public pools
they used this ditch often.
In August, 1942, the body of Jose Diaz
was found near the ditch;
his skull had been crushed.
Twenty-two Mexican-Americans were arrested
and charged with murder.
Twelve of the defendants were found guilty of murder,
five of assault.
The evidence against them was so flimsy
their convictions were overturned by the District Court of Appeals;
but not before eight of the young men had served
nearly two years in San Quentin.

5

In May, 1943,
teenage Anglos egged on by sailors
chased a group of Mexican-Americans
out of the Aragon ballroom at Ocean Park
and started a riot
that surged up the beach from Venice to Santa Monica.
"The only thing we could do to break it up,"
said a police officer,
"was to arrest Mexican kids."

6

Thursday night, June 3, 1943,
eleven sailors walking along North Main Street
were attacked by zoot-suiters.
The next night
100 sailors armed with clubs and blackjacks
hired 20 taxicabs
and drove to the Mexican district
on the east side of Los Angeles
and beat up every zoot-suiter they could find.
They broke into beer joints and restaurants
and dragged boys from their seats
and ripped off their suits and clubbed them.
Police arrested nine sailors;
all were released without charges.

7

Next day sailors and soldiers and marines
hurried to Los Angeles on weekend passes.
That night they roamed
through the *barrios*
warning *pachucos* to get rid of their suits
in 24 hours.
Sunday night, June 6,
servicemen swept through the streets
pulling *pachuco* and Negro zootsuiters
out of restaurants and streetcars
and stripping them
and beating them with clubs.
Police made 44 arrests. All were *pachucos*
and all were badly mauled.

8

Next morning the riots crowded the war news off the front pages. Said the **Eagle Rock Advertiser**: "Most of the citizens of the city have been delighted with what has been going on."

9

Monday night civilians joined the attack.
Cabdrivers offered free rides to the *barrios*.
Thousands of soldiers and sailors and citizens
stormed through the streets
waving bottles and blackjacks.
Traffic crunched to a halt;
the attackers ripped through bars and dancehalls.
They forced theatre owners to turn up the houselights
while they searched the aisles.
They broke into homes
and grabbed boys and beat them
while their mothers pleaded for their lives.
Police made little effort to halt the rampage.
Four *pachucos* emerging from a poolhall
were apprehended. A boy with a wooden leg resisted.
"Why am I being arrested?" he cried.
A policeman cracked a stick over his head
and kicked him in the face when he fell.

10

Tuesday, June 8,
federal troops were called in to restore order.
The Navy ruled Los Angeles off-limits.
Race riots broke out in Detroit and New York.
The Mexican ambassador
demanded a formal explanation from the State Department.
In Germany
Joseph Goebbels went on radio
to denounce the discrepancy
between American ideals
and American actions.

Harry Truman Takes a Walk

Harry Truman buttons his coat, adjusts his hat, takes hold of his cane, and steps out. Step step step, 120 per minute, one right after the other, heels clicking evenly along the pavement, clip clip clip. He walks like he's been at it for centuries, a brisk, stiff-legged cadence, arms swinging with metronomic precision, swish swish swish, 120 beats per minute. Down Pennsylvania Avenue, down Madison Avenue, down Whitehead Street in Key West, through the rubble of Potsdam, toward MacArthur's waiting aircraft on Wake Island, to the library at Independence.

Harry Truman walks hard. His blood surges through his veins. His heart swells with vigor. His fingers bulge like turnips. His cheeks glow pink and seraphic. His eyes glitter behind rimless lenses. His breath escapes in quick blasts like an old-time thresher.

Harry Truman walks everywhere. He strides across the farm hustling cattle to pasture. He strides across France firing cannon at the Boche. He strides across Jackson County laying concrete for new roads. He strides through Congress cutting fat from the budget. He strides across the convention floor to accept the Democratic nomination. He strides to Korea to hold back the Communists.

Harry Truman walks without braces. Harry Truman walks without crutches. The crippled president is dead. A new one with bonafide legs takes power. He walks up trees, he walks up waterfalls, he walks up the side of the Capitol rotunda. He walks everywhere at a furious pace that leaves reporters gasping. Quick answers to quick questions, enunciated without hesitation, 120 beats per minute, tappa ta ta, tappa ta ta, tappa ta ta. Syllables riveting the air.

Faces crowd the curb as he passes. Hello Averell, Hello Dean, Hello Bess, Hello Alben, Hello Winston, Hello Clement, Hello Margaret, Hello George, Hello Eddie, Hello Louis, Hello Doug, Hello Mom, Hello Dwight, Hello Joe, Hello Henry. They smile and wave, he smiles and waves. They tap their toes, he taps his toes and does a speedy hambone shuffle. They all do a speedy hambone shuffle, the whole nation does a speedy hambone shuffle, smacking their heels against the pavement, ragga cha cha, ragga cha cha, ragga cha cha, a rapid syncopated beat that pulses through the ionosphere and illuminates the heavens with a peculiarly American glow. Harry Truman walks hard, he has the magic gait.

All are mesmerized by the rhythmic pace of Harry's wingtips. All are drawn into his churning wake. The suction is greater than a sinking battleship. Egos flounder, personalities dissolve. Waterwings are of little use; corklined underwear is a needless extravagance. Diplomats, druggists, shoeshine boys, senators, chauffeurs, secretaries, infielders, janitors, movie extras, are swept up. Some float, some drown, all feel the tug, the irresistible pull. Shadows on the ruins at Hiroshima unlimber their frigid silhouettes; the dead at Buchenwald rise up with a grin; casualties on Okinawa wade back out to their ships.

Harry Truman walks down 12th Street, Harry Truman walks down Fifth Avenue, Harry Truman walks down the Champs Élysées, Harry Truman walks down Wilshire Boulevard. The world is alerted to a new pace, a farmboy wobble tempered by military training, animated by raw energy, the metabolism of a nation. Unhindered by self-consciousness, unfettered by doubt, unimpeded by introspection, a quick instinctive step, the motion of a buffalo toward a water hole, a jaguar toward its prey. The last free step of the century, the culmination of a long line of pioneer steppers, Manifest Destiny of the arches.

Harry Truman walks to the Yalu, Harry Truman walks through Greece, Harry Truman walks around Berlin. Harry Truman walks the route his corpuscles have programmed, without pause, without faltering. Harry Truman walks through the final act of a fabulous tragi-comedy, the thrust of three centuries, right off the stage, into the wings. Moths swell like robins, starlings cackle imperiously. The clip clip clip of his cat's-paw heels can be heard on every pavement in America. He parts wreaths of automobile fumes easier than Moses the Red Sea waves. General Sherman grins with envy; Francis Parkman takes notes. The rhythm is insatiable, the rhythm is overwhelming, the rhythm is stupendous. Landscapes flatten, hills collapse, trees shed leaves, the sun slips shyly out of sight. Tidewater, Appalachia, riverine network, ineffable plains, granitic mountains, alkali basins, balmy coast range, soft Pacific waters feel the pressure of his marching feet.

Harry Truman walks on the moon, Harry Truman walks on Mars, Harry Truman walks across the Antilles, stepping surefootedly from island to island. *No one will ever walk like him again.* Muscles wilt, limbs grow spavined, energy is rerouted. After three centuries of westerly progression Harry's path turns inward, to the parameters of the psyche, the incubus of the self. Silently Harry's energy winds down with entropic certainty, erg by erg, to a cinder, a dried peel. Silently Harry comes to a FULL STOP on a sandy spit near Key West. Silently he entombs his feet in a sepulcher of conch shells. Silently he launches his cane on an ocean of sympathetic memory. Silently he passes into the air, a Gulf Stream scent, borne by roiling breezes toward the outer distances.

Harry Truman floats in heaven, Harry Truman floats on earth, Harry Truman floats the fathomless spaces of death, alone, unaided, unabetted, holding his feet in his hands, cradling his heels in his arms, muttering doxological refrains, 120 beats per minute, pumped out in a droll twang, wasah sassah sah, wasah sassah sah, wasah sassah sah. His shoes leave no imprint in the aery wastes. His heart frosts. His eyes hang vacantly in his face. His cheeks become transparent. The light goes out, the itch, the folksy urging. He settles down, another speck in the Van Allen belt, invisible infinitesimal inconsequential, the echo of his footsteps blending indistinguishably with the hubbub of his dreams.

Over DeSoto's Bones:
An Initiation Story

Went by inner tube
Hayti down to Natchez

(tight-assed, in a dither
lips crimped to a stony pout)

skimming over Father Muddy's
curdly top; river of tawny brawn

surface etched in curdles
fat sun kissing the foam.

Past Helena a blue heron advised
pull up my heels lest they be clipped

by guardian fish. Of what? I retorted;
Spanish doubloons, Fort Knox gold?

Your sass is misapplied, said he;
these bones you are glissading over

belong to old Hernando
sacred to crayfish & cat alike

buffalo carp & alligator gar:
everything that squiggles underneath

or respires. Harumph! said I
& no sooner than a stick

punctured my tube
& with a flatulent hiss

I slipped under. A smarmy
sepia world it was

like a liquid Mathew Brady print;
old gars in butternut

dudy carp in pantaloons
nudged me friendily:

Hello there, Howdy, Welcome Aboard!
Deeper I plopped through chocolate slop

past ironclads, sternwheelers
niggers hobbled at the neck

with iron rings:
How far you come? Plannin to stay long?

Where weeds should have grown
sprayed a field of bones

sarcophageal white
as an elephant graveyard

sparkling bones that stretched downstream
in a beckoning path;

presided over by a bearded skull
helmeted with rusty plate.

W...E...L...C...O...M...E
cranked the jaw;

you have entered the oldest country,
an infernal region of memory

& desire. Perhaps you thought
you were in Hell?

Laughter unhinged the jaw.
My bones decanted & floated free

in the company of slimy tongues
that slicked the joints

so they could never link again.
YOU COMFORTABLE, BOY?

the voice queried
with mock solicitousness.

All my bones answered at once
a chorusing archipelago

that reverberated upstream & down
knocking fish offcourse & rousing soggy eels:

"Whatever happens, happens...."
(lips unfurling

in a confident grin).
SHAZAM, BOY! Hernando boomed

& instantly each bone ignited like an albino eye
lighting up this murky world

a hundred different myriad lights
for me, at least, to see.

Conger Beasley, Jr. was born in St. Joseph, Missouri, and was educated in Connecticut and New York City. He is the author of two published novels, **Hidalgo's Beard: A California Fantasy** *(1979) and* **The Ptomaine Kid: A Hamburger Western** *(1981). Inspiration for the poems published in* **Over DeSoto's Bones** *came from ten years' travel and residence in the American Southwest and Mexico. Mr. Beasley resides in Kansas City, where he is presently completing a volume of short stories.*

Ahsahta Press

POETRY OF THE WEST

MODERN

*Norman Macleod, *Selected Poems*
 Gwendolen Haste, *Selected Poems*
*Peggy Pond Church, *New & Selected Poems*
 Haniel Long, *My Seasons*
 H. L. Davis, *Selected Poems*
*Hildegarde Flanner, *The Hearkening Eye*
 Genevieve Taggard, *To the Natural World*
 Hazel Hall, *Selected Poems*
 Women Poets of the West: An Anthology
*Thomas Hornsby Ferril, *Anvil of Roses*
*Judson Crews, *The Clock of Moss*

CONTEMPORARY

*Marnie Walsh, *A Taste of the Knife*
*Robert Krieger, *Headlands, Rising*
 Richard Blessing, *Winter Constellations*
*Carolyne Wright, *Stealing the Children*
 Charley John Greasybear, *Songs*
*Conger Beasley, Jr., *Over DeSoto's Bones*
*Susan Strayer Deal, *No Moving Parts*
*Gretel Ehrlich, *To Touch the Water*
*Leo Romero, *Agua Negra*
*David Baker, *Laws of the Land*
*Richard Speakes, *Hannah's Travel*
 Dixie Partridge, *Deer in the Haystacks*

*Selections from these volumes, read by their authors, are now available
 on *The Ahsahta Cassette Sampler*.